Sermon Outli

SERMON OUTLINES *for* REVELATION

Message Outlines Prepared for the Study of God's Word

In the Book of the Revelation of Jesus Christ

JON J. CARDWELL

SERMON OUTLINES FOR REVELATION

Copyright ©2012 by Jon J. Cardwell. All rights reserved.

All scripture is quoted from the King James Version of the Holy Bible. The King James Version is in the Public Domain.

Scripture quotations marked (ESV) are from The Holy Bible, English Standard Version, copyright ©2001 by Crossway Bibles, a publishing ministry of Good News Publishers. Used by permission. All rights reserved.

Cover designs and internal art by Jon J. Cardwell ©2012

Published by *Vayahiy Press*   vayahiypress.com

Printed by Create Space in the United States of America.

*For Jesus Christ, our Lord;
for all He is and all He does*

CONTENTS

1. The Revelation of Jesus Christ — 1
2. Unto His Servant John — 5
3. Sent and Signified — 9
4. Thou Art Worthy, O Lord — Outline 1 — 15
5. Revelation Chapter One — Outline 2 — 17
6. Christ, Our Sufficiency — Outline 3 — 19
7. Christ, Our Eternal Reward — Outline 4 — 23
8. The Revelation of St. John the Divine — Outline 5 — 27
9. Sea of Glass — Outline 6 — 29
10. The Lamb Opens the Seals — Outline 7 — 33
11. The Praise of Sovereign Grace — Outline 8 — 37
12. Woe, Woe, Woe — Outline 9 — 39
13. The Gospel Witness — Outline 10 — 41
14. A Wonder in Heaven — Outline 11 — 43
15. The Mark of the Beast — Outline 12 — 47
16. The Lamb Slain — Outline 13 — 51

17. The Lamb on the Mount Sion — Outline 14 — 53
18. The Lamb's Harvest — Outline 15 — 57
19. The Wrath of God — Outline 16 — 61
20. Seven Vials & Mystery Babylon — Outline 17 — 65
21. Mystery Babylon & the Beast — Outline 18 — 69
22. Babylon is Fallen — Outline 19 — 73
23. Two Suppers — Outline 20 — 75
24. The Testimony of Jesus — Outline 21 — 79
25. Two Resurrections — Outline 22 — 81
About the Author — 85
Fiction for Youth — 87
Coming Soon — 89

Chapter One

The Revelation of Jesus Christ

"The Revelation of Jesus Christ, which God gave unto him, to shew unto his servants things which must shortly come to pass; and he sent and signified it by his angel unto his servant John:"

Revelation 1:1

THE FIRST AND MOST IMPORTANT truth to consider about this book of the Bible is that it is the revelation of Jesus Christ. Written in the book of Revelation is the apocalypse, the unveiling of Jesus Christ. As the Alpha and Omega, Jesus Christ is the first and the last in all things, and the first and foremost of and among all things. My Bible, a large print Presentation Reference Edition of the King James Version published by Cambridge University Press, renders the title of this book: "THE REVELATION OF ST. JOHN THE DIVINE." Many Bibles give this book that title. Yet, it may be more appropriately rendered, "The Revelation of Jesus Christ." Every jot and title of the writings of the book of Revelation contain the essence of the Person of Christ and the work of Christ; in other words, the gospel.

The doctrine contained within this last book of the Bible is centered in the gospel of Jesus Christ, His eternal sacrifice as the Lamb of God, His eternal rule as the Lion of the tribe of Judah, and the church He has built and is building in the kingdom of God. It must be this way because the gospel of Jesus Christ is the central doctrine for every book of the Bible. If any book of the Bible is interpreted apart from the central truths contained in the Person and work of Jesus Christ, then all other doctrine, devotion, and duty will tend toward error and sin. Any interpretation of scripture that isn't centered in the gospel of Jesus Christ, in my humble opinion is, in fact, anti-Christ.

The revelation, the unveiling, the apocalypse, and the disclosure of Jesus Christ will produce worship in the souls of His saints. When Jesus spoke words of truth to the woman drawing water at the well of Samaria, He said, *"But the hour cometh, and now is, when the true worshippers shall worship the Father in spirit and in truth: for the Father seeketh such to worship him"* (John 4:23). Throughout this book we see the magnificent worship of the people of God:

—John was *"in the Spirit on the Lord's day."* Revelation 1:10
—John was *"immediately in the spirit..."* Revelation 4:2
—The four beasts *"rest not day and not"* in their worship around the throne of Christ. Revelation 4:8, 9
—The twenty-four elders *"fall down before [Christ sitting upon His] throne, and worship him... and cast their crowns before the throne..."* Revelation 4:10
—Jesus Christ is worshipped throughout Revelation 5 as the Lion of Judah, the Root of David, and the Lamb Slain.

Sermon Outlines for Revelation

— There is hopeful worship in the midst of tribulation among the souls of saints *"under the altar."* Revelation 6:9, 10

— The Lamb of God is worshipped by an innumerable multitude with white robes and palm branches in Revelation 7:9, 10.

— We see again the worship of God by the entire heavenly host in Revelation 7:11-12.

— We see the worship in catechism form by questions and revelation of truth in Revelation 7:13-17.

— There is the worship of God through the smoke of incense and the prayers of saints in Revelation 8:3, 4.

— There is the worship of God by his prophetic Word through anointed men proclaiming the eternal gospel of Jesus Christ before *"many peoples, and nations, and tongues, and kings."* Revelation 10:9-11

— The worshippers, as the temple of the living God are measured in the opening of Revelation 11 and at the close of the chapter, the 24 elders, once again, fall upon their faces and worship God.

— In Revelation 12, we read of the worship led by *"a loud voice...in heaven"* proclaiming with power the powerful gospel of Jesus Christ. Revelation 12:10-12

— Revelation 13 identifies the trials and tribulations that true spiritual worshippers of Christ will face (Revelation 13:7-9) amidst the summit of fallen man's pride, the extent of fallen man's wisdom, and the depth of fallen man's depravity.

— Revelation 14 begins with the purity of worship among the followers of the Lamb, and ends with the heavenly worship of *"the everlasting gospel [preached] unto them that dwell on the earth"* to command sinners to fear God and worship Him, for judgment is coming.

The Revelation of Jesus Christ

— In Revelation 15, those who *"had gotten victory over the beast, and over his image, and over his mark, and over the number of his name"* stand upon a sea of glass and worship God with harps, singing the song of Moses; and the temple of God was filled with the smoke of God's glory.

— Revelation 16:15 presents the worship of God through the benediction to His people amidst the judgments of God upon those who reject the glory of God in Christ Jesus our Lord.

— Revelation 17:7-18 presents the worship of God through the exposition of His Word by the illumination of the Spirit through anointed messengers (angels).

— In Revelation 18 there is also a contrasting difference between the worship of the Lord's saints expressed throughout the book, and the worship of the world by the sinful, wicked world, which shall be judged by the Almighty in the end.

— Revelation 19 presents the worship of God throughout the chapter.

— Revelation 20 presents the worship of God in His righteous judgments.

— Revelation 21-21 presents the ultimate worship of God's people when His glorious plan is ultimately fulfilled in the new heaven and new earth.

If we have failed to see the blessedness of the worship of Christ revealed in the book of Revelation, we've failed to truly see Christ in the scriptures contained therein.

Chapter Two

Unto His Servant John

"The Revelation of Jesus Christ, which God gave unto him, to shew unto his servants things which must shortly come to pass; and he sent and signified it by his angel unto his servant John:"

Revelation 1:1

YES, THIS BOOK IS the revelation of Jesus Christ; it is all about the Lord; and its writings unveil Him and magnify Him; nevertheless, we can clearly say that the Lord's servant, John, penned the words to this book. Just as Paul dictated to Tertius (Romans 16:22) and others, John was a scribe for the actual author, Jesus Christ.

Which John are we talking about? Who was the scribe that the Lord Jesus sent and signified the revelation of Himself unto? The external evidence is almost entirely unanimous in its support of the apostle and gospel writer who leaned upon the Lord's breast at the Last Supper in John 13. The internal evidence, if not overwhelming, is not unfavorable to John as the author. Additionally, the gospel of John, the epistle of 1

John, and the book of Revelation are the only writings of the New Testament that refer to Jesus as ο λογος (*ho logos*), "the Word" (John 1:1, 14; 1 John 1:1;[1] Revelation 19:13). If the scribe is indeed the beloved disciple, we might also see through the writings of John the signature of the Holy Spirit as God presents to us a beautiful pattern from a panoramic view of the New Testament messages given by this particular servant:

THE GOSPEL: Written That We Might Believe…

"But these are written, that ye might believe that Jesus is the Christ, the Son of God; and that believing ye might have life through His name." John 20:31

THE EPISTLES: Written That We Might Be Sure…

"These things have I written unto you that believe on the name of the Son of God; that ye may know that ye have eternal life, and that ye may believe on the name of the Son of God." 1 John 5:13

THE REVELATION: Written That We Might Be Steadfast…

"And He saith unto me, Seal not the sayings of the prophecy of this book: for the time is at hand." Revelation 22:10

The Divine Purpose of Revelation is not to enlighten us about future events. The primary purpose of this book is to

---

[1] 1 John 1:1, περι του λογου της ζωης (*peri tou logou tes zoes*), "of the word of life."

Sermon Outlines for Revelation

ENCOUNTER JESUS PERSONALLY; to have a deeper intimacy with our Lord and Savior because the words of this prophecy reveal Him, unveil Him, and disclose Him: "for the testimony of Jesus is the spirit of prophecy" (Revelation 19:10).

The Divine Message of Revelation is that the almighty King is sitting on His throne, He is in control, and He is coming soon!

The Divine Blessing of Revelation comes implicitly because of the divine purpose of the book, as well as the divine message of the book; yet, it is also spelled out explicitly that the reading, hearing and heeding of the words of this book will result in a blessing:

"Blessed is he that readeth, and they that hear the words of this prophecy, and keep those things which are written therein: for the time is at hand." Revelation 1:3

"Behold, I come quickly: blessed is he that keepeth the sayings of the prophecy of this book." Revelation 22:7

You may be wondering why I've skipped over the portion that says that the Lord Jesus *"sent and signified it by his angel."* We will actually look at that in our next chapter, and once you've read it, you'll know why we covered this information about John's part in the writing of Revelation first.

Chapter Three

Sent and Signified

"The Revelation of Jesus Christ, which God gave unto him, to shew unto his servants things which must shortly come to pass; and he sent and signified it by his angel unto his servant John:"

Revelation 1:1

THIS MESSAGE OF the revealed Christ, the unveiled Christ, the disclosure of Christ, was not only sent by the Lord's messenger to John, but it was set in signs; that it was significantly symbolized. How is this revelation of Christ symbolized? I suggest that it is symbolized in two significant ways: (1) who Jesus Christ is; and (2) what Jesus Christ has done; specifically and more importantly, His atoning death upon Calvary's cross.

As I mentioned in our last chapter, "Unto His Servant John," given the evidence at hand, it appears that John the gospel writer is the very same author of this particular book, The Revelation of Jesus Christ. If we work under that assumption, some of the symbolism seems to fit in the book of

Revelation's expressions with those expressed in the Gospel According to John.

Significant Symbolism in Christ's Person. In both the Gospel According to John and the Revelation of Jesus Christ we see significant symbolism in who Jesus Christ is:

As Jesus Christ is the eternal Word made flesh through His incarnation in John's gospel (John 1:1, 14), *"his name is called the Word of God"* in Christ's return *"clothed with a vesture dipped in blood"* in the apocalypse (Revelation 19:13, ESV).

As Jesus Christ is *"the Lamb of God, who takes away the sin of the world"* in John's gospel (John 1:29, ESV), we also see Christ as *"a Lamb standing, as though it had been slain"* (Revelation 5:6, ESV), and throughout the entire book of Revelation.

As Jesus Christ is the Bread of Life that nourishes His people in John's gospel (John 6:35), we also see Christ as the Hidden Manna promised to His church for food in the apocalypse (Revelation 2:17).

As Jesus Christ is the Light of the World in John's gospel (John 8:12), we also see Christ as the Lamb illuminating the new heaven and earth in the apocalypse (Revelation 21:23).

As Jesus Christ is the True Vine and His disciples are the fruit-bearing branches in John's gospel (John 15:1, 5), we also see Christ as the Vine in the apocalypse, and the fruit of the branches abiding in the Vine of Christ is harvested (Revelation 14:18).

There is much more that can be said of who Jesus Christ than this; yet, to exhaust our language in describing Christ and expressing His person would not even skim the surface of His unfathomable depth or bring us even a cubit closer in scaling His unreachable height. Nevertheless, His people can know Him for He has revealed Himself to each one of us, in terms that are accessible, knowledge that is attainable, and perspective that is understandable. The transcendent God of creation is full of compassion for His creatures and does not say to us, "You must serve Me, but you cannot know anything about Me." Neither does He say to us, "Have a relationship with Me, but you cannot know Me." Though our finite minds cannot ascend, attain, or entertain the infinite truths of God, we can know them within the confines of our limited intellect because He has revealed Himself to us:

"The secret things belong unto the LORD our God: but those things which are revealed belong unto us and to our children for ever, that we may do all the words of this law." Deuteronomy 29:29

Yet, to know about Christ, even ascending to the glorious truths of His majesty and splendor as God, or His holiness and righteousness in sinless perfection as Man, does not mean that we really know Christ unless we know Him through His atoning work of redemption in His sacrificial death upon Calvary's tree. There is no way that anyone can know Him in an intimate personal relationship as we have been made adopted sons of His Father nor can we know Christ as brother unless we have been reconciled to Him through His redeeming blood, His propitiating grace, and His expiating mercy. The majesty, the supremacy, the holiness, and the superlative excellence of the atoning death of Jesus Christ is not and cannot be divorced from who He is. The person and the work of Christ are inseparable and you cannot look at one without the other. If we are not captivated by the embrace of grace through the cross of Jesus Christ, then the majesty, supremacy, the holiness, and the superlative excellence of the person of Jesus Christ is silly sentimentality.

The death, burial, and resurrection of Christ are part and parcel of all that is Christ. All His holy and righteous teachings, miracles and healings would have been for naught had He not gone to the cross. The sum and substance of all wisdom in

truth may be found in Christ's words to Pontius Pilate when Jesus said, *"You say that I am a king. For this purpose I was born and for this purpose I have come into the world — to bear witness to the truth. Everyone who is of the truth listens to my voice"* (John 18:37, ESV). This is why Christ came. It is the very central truth for all humanity; for if not for the cross of Christ, the question of how a sinful man can stand rightly before a holy God can never be answered. Without the supremacy and sovereignty of Jesus Christ's atoning work upon the cross of Calvary is to remove the supremacy and sovereignty of the nature and character of Christ's person.

Significant Symbolism in Christ's Atoning Work. In the Gospel According to John we are told of the significance of Christ's death. In three places in particular John uses the word "signifying," which is the same Greek root word translated "signified" in Revelation 1:1. What is specifically significant about this word "signified" in John's gospel is that each time it is pointing to the crucifixion; and two out of those three times it specifically speaks of Christ's own crucifixion:

"And I, if I be lifted up from the earth, will draw all men unto me. This he said, signifying what death he should die." John 12:32-33

"Then said Pilate unto them, Take ye him, and judge him according to your law. The Jews therefore said unto him, It is not lawful for us to put any man to death: That the saying of Jesus might be fulfilled, which he spake, signifying what death he should die." John 18:31-32

In the Revelation of Jesus Christ we see significant symbolism presented in Christ's atoning work upon the cross. Here are just a few references:

SERMON OUTLINES FOR REVELATION

"And from Jesus Christ, who is the faithful witness, and the first begotten of the dead, and the prince of the kings of the earth. Unto him that loved us, and washed us from our sins in his own blood," Revelation 1:5

"And they sung a new song, saying, Thou art worthy to take the book, and to open the seals thereof: for thou wast slain, and hast redeemed us to God by thy blood out of every kindred, and tongue, and people, and nation;" Revelation 5:9

"Saying with a loud voice, Worthy is the Lamb that was slain to receive power, and riches, and wisdom, and strength, and honour, and glory, and blessing." Revelation 5:12

"And they overcame Him by the blood of the Lamb, and by the word of their testimony; and they loved not their lives unto the death." Revelation 12:11

"And all that dwell upon the earth shall worship him, whose names are not written in the book of life of the Lamb slain from the foundation of the world." Revelation 13:8

The book of the Revelation of Jesus Christ is symbolized in, by and through the gospel of the Lord Jesus Christ. In the outlines contained in this work, they were preached from what I would call an "Idealist View." In other words, the symbols are symbolic of that which pertains to the gospel of Jesus Christ in one way, shape or form. I believe that a significant rise in liberalism and liberal theology at the turn of the twentieth century actually hijacked the symbolism in the Book of Revelation in order to satisfy personal lusts that would naturally spring forth from the flesh under a liberal theology. Symbols became subjective as they were interpreted by

personal prejudices and perspectives. Interpreting symbols objectively by the gospel of Jesus Christ were thrown out the window by liberal thinking and academia. As a result, idealism in the interpretation of Revelation was shunned by more conservative and orthodox theologians.

It is my prayer that a true and Biblical idealist view will be recaptured by pastors, preachers and ministers of the gospel, and regardless of one's eschatology, that the gospel of Jesus Christ, His Person and atoning work, will be first and last, prominent and predominant, with all glory unto God the Father, in all that we think, say and do. May these outlines in the Book of Revelation help to serve unto that end. Amen.

Outline One

REVELATION 1-7 Overview

I. INTRODUCTION

    1. Revelation of Jesus Christ
       — the gospel supremely expressed

    2. Revelation of St. John the Divine
       — the gospel submissively possessed

II. CHAPTER ONE

    1. Jesus Christ: Universal & Preeminent Truth, vv1-3
       — A Theological Perspective

    2. Jesus Christ: Personal & Redemptive Truth, vv4-6
       — A Soteriological Perspective

    3. Jesus Christ: Functional & Testimonial Truth, vv7-20
       — An Ecclesiological Perspective

Thou Art Worthy, O Lord

III. CHAPTERS TWO & THREE

    1. Christ, Our Sufficiency

    2. Christ, Our Reward

    3. Judgment Begins in the House of the Lord

IV. CHAPTERS FOUR & FIVE

    1. The Wonder of Heaven, Ch.4

    2. The Worship of Heaven, Ch.5

        a. Sealed Word reveals the Lamb slain, vv1-7

        b. Word in the hand of the sovereign Lamb produces prayer, v8

        c. Precious prayer before the throne produces praise, vv9-14

V. CHAPTERS SIX & SEVEN

    1. Revelation of Christ in the Fall of Man, Seals 1-4

    2. Blood of the Prophets in Preaching Christ, Seal 5

    3. Crucifixion, Resurrection, Judgment of Cross, Seal 6a

    4. Salvations from the Cross, Seal 6b (Ch.7)

Outline Two

Revelation Chapter One

I. INTRODUCTION

    1. Acts of the Apostles

        —Christ's Messengers to His Body
        The Work of the Redeemer through His Subjects

    2. Revelation of Jesus Christ
        —Christ's Message for His Bride
        The Word of the Redeemer in His Reign

II. CHAPTER BREAKDOWN

    1. Jesus Christ: Universal & Preeminent Truth, vv1-3

        —Theological

    2. Jesus Christ: Personal & Redemptive Truth, vv4-6

        —Soteriological

3. Jesus Christ: Functional & Testimonial Truth, vv7-20

— Ecclesiological

III. KEYS TO UNLOCKING THE BOOK

1. The Lord Shown (Revelation)

2. The Lamb Slain (Redemption)

3. The Light Supreme (Reign)

IV. APPLICATION OF THIS TRUTH

1. A Blessed Reader

2. A Discerning Hearer

3. A Faithful Keeper

Outline Three

Christ, Our Sufficiency

I. INTRODUCTION

Preeminence & Priorities from our Divine Outline:

>1. Christ in Revelation
>   — The Lord Seen (Prophet), Rev 1:1-3
>
>2. Christ in Salvation
>   — The Lamb Slain (Priest), Rev 1:4-6
>
>3. Christ in Sanctification
>   — The Light Supreme (King), Rev 1:7-20

Passage for our Outline Selection

>**Revelation 2:1-3:22**

II. THE SEVEN CHURCHES

>1. Ephesus: Church Left First Love

> Jesus Christ: "*He that holdeth the seven stars in his right hand, who walketh in the midst of the seven golden candlesticks;*"
>
> Christ is our Sufficiency: His loving presence is eternally abiding

2. Smyrna: Church Suffered Tribulation unto Death

> Jesus Christ: "*the first and the last, which was dead, and is alive.*"
>
> Christ is our Sufficiency: He is the resurrection and the life in will raise the believer in the last day

3. Pergamos: Church of Compromise

> Jesus Christ: "*he which hath the sharp sword with two edges.*"
>
> Christ is our Sufficiency: He is the living, uncompromised Word of life

4. Thyatira: Covetous Church (Idolatry & Fornication)

> Jesus Christ: "*the Son of God, who hath his eyes like unto a flame of fire, and his feet are like fine brass.*"
>
> Christ is our Sufficiency: He is the true high priest and eternal God, our delight and desire

5. Sardis: Church of Hypocrisy

Jesus Christ: *"he that hath the seven Spirits of God, and the seven stars."*

Christ is our Sufficiency: Honesty and humility is His through His Holy Spirit by His holy messengers

6. Philadelphia: Church with Little Strength, 1 Cor 1:26

Jesus Christ: *"he that is holy, he that is true, he that hath the key of David, he that openeth, and no man shutteth; and shutteth, and no man openeth."*

Christ is our Sufficiency: All power is His to reveal, to call, to save, and to sanctify

7. Laodiceans: Church of Complacency

Jesus Christ: *"the Amen, the faithful and true witness, the beginning of the creation of God."*

Christ is our Sufficiency: All things begin and end with Christ, so apart from Him we have nothing, and are nothing

III. CONCLUDING COMMENTS

1. A Personal Word, *"He that hath an ear, let him hear…"*

2. A Corporate Word, *"what the Spirit saith unto the churches;"*

Outline Four

Christ, Our Eternal Reward

I. INTRODUCTION

Preeminence & Priorities from our Divine Outline:

    1. Christ in Revelation
       — The Lord Seen (Prophet), Rev 1:1-3

    2. Christ in Salvation
       — The Lamb Slain (Priest), Rev 1:4-6

    3. Christ in Sanctification
       — The Light Supreme (King), Rev 1:7-20

Passage for our Outline Selection

    Revelation 2:1-3:22

II. THE SEVEN CHURCHES

    1. Ephesus: Church Left First Love

Jesus Christ: *"To him that overcometh will I give to eat of the tree of life, which is in the midst of the paradise of God."* 2:7

Christ is our Reward: *"I am the living bread which came down from heaven: if any man eat of this bread, he shall live for ever: and the bread that I will give is my flesh, which I will give for the life of the world."* John 6:51

2. Smyrna: Church Suffered Tribulation unto Death

Jesus Christ: *"He that overcometh shall not be hurt of the second death."* 2:11

Christ is our Reward: *"I am the resurrection, and the life: he that believeth in me, though he were dead, yet shall he live:"* John 11:25

3. Pergamos: Church of Compromise

Jesus Christ: *"To him that overcometh will I give to eat of the hidden manna, and will give him a white stone, and in the stone a new name written, which no man knoweth saving he that receiveth it."* 2:17

Christ is our Reward: *"And he that sat was to look upon like a jasper and a sardine stone"* Revelation 4:3

4. Thyatira: Covetous Church (Idolatry & Fornication)

Jesus Christ: *"And I will give him the morning star."* 2:28

Sermon Outlines for Revelation

Christ is our Reward: *"I am the root and the offspring of David, and the bright and morning star."* Revelation 22:16

5. Sardis: Church of Hypocrisy

   Jesus Christ: *"He that overcometh, the same shall be clothed in white raiment; and I will not blot out his name out of the book of life, but I will confess his name before my Father, and before his angels."* 3:5

   Christ is our Reward: *"I am the way, the truth, and the life: no man cometh unto the Father, but by me."* John 14:6

6. Philadelphia: Church with Little Strength, 1 Cor 1:26

   Jesus Christ: *"Him that overcometh will I make a pillar in the temple of my God, and he shall go no more out: and I will write upon him the name of my God, and the name of the city of my God, which is new Jerusalem, which cometh down out of heaven from my God: and I will write upon him my new name."* 3:12

   Christ is our Reward: *"Behold, I have graven thee upon the palms of my hands; thy walls are continually before me."* Isaiah 49:16

7. Laodiceans: Church of Complacency

   Jesus Christ: *"To him that overcometh will I grant to sit with me in my throne, even as I also overcame, and am set down with my Father in his throne."* 3:21

Christ, Our Eternal Reward

Christ is our Reward: "*Fear not, Abram: I am thy shield, and thy exceeding great reward.*" Genesis 15:1

III. CONCLUDING COMMENTS

"*Nevertheless I am continually with thee: thou hast holden me by my right hand. Thou shalt guide me with thy counsel, and afterward receive me to glory. Whom have I in heaven but thee? and there is none upon earth that I desire beside thee. My flesh and my heart faileth: but God is the strength of my heart, and my portion for ever.*" Psalms 73:23-26

"*The LORD is the portion of mine inheritance and of my cup: thou maintainest my lot.*" Psalms 16:5

"*I cried unto thee, O LORD: I said, Thou art my refuge and my portion in the land of the living.*" Psalms 142:5

"*The LORD is my portion, saith my soul; therefore will I hope in him.*" Lamentations 3:24

"*Therefore let no man glory in men. For all things are yours; Whether Paul, or Apollos, or Cephas, or the world, or life, or death, or things present, or things to come; all are yours; And ye are Christ's; and Christ is God's.*" 1 Corinthians 3:21-23

Outline Five

The Revelation of St. John the Divine

I. INTRODUCTION

Preeminence & Priorities from our Divine Outline:

1. Christ in Revelation
   — The Lord Seen (Prophet), Rev 1:1-3

2. Christ in Salvation
   — The Lamb Slain (Priest), Rev 1:4-6

3. Christ in Sanctification
   — The Light Supreme (King), Rev 1:7-20

The title of the message:

"The Revelation of St. John the Divine"

The revelation, revealing, unveiling of Jesus Christ, to the saints of God in Christ, is a personal revelation, since Christ is the believer's Sufficiency and Reward

Passage for our Outline Selection
Revelation 4:1-5:14

II. THE WONDER OF HEAVEN, REVELATION 4

Μετα ταυτα ("After this"), v1
The term occurs in Revelation 4:1; 7:1; 7:9; 9:2; 15:5; 18:1; 19:1

    1. What we see of heaven as John describes it:

    —The Open Door, v1 (contrast with Rev 3:20-22)

    —The Throne of Christ, vv1-3

    —The Twenty-four Elders, v4

    —The Seven Spirits, v5

    —The Sea of Glass, v6

    —The Four Beasts, vv6-9

    —Holy, Holy, Holy, vv10-11

III. THE WORSHIP OF HEAVEN – REVELATION 5

    —The Sealed Book, vv1-4

    —The Lamb Slain, vv5-7

    —The Prayers of Saints, vv8-10

    —The Worship of the Lamb, vv11-14

Outline Six

Sea of Glass

I. REVELATION 4:6

"And before the throne there was a sea of glass like unto crystal: and in the midst of the throne, and round about the throne, were four beasts full of eyes before and behind."

Access to the throne of Christ is by the Sea of Glass, which is before the throne: the Sea of Glass is the Gospel Message; of who Christ is, of all He has done, and its effectual power to carry out God's eternal plans and purposes

II. A SEA OF GLASS: THE GOSPEL MESSAGE

    1. A Sea of Purifying Judgment
And I saw as it were a sea of glass <u>mingled with fire</u>: and them that had gotten the victory over the beast, and over his image, and over his mark, and over the number of his name, stand on the sea of glass, having the harps of God." Revelation 15:2

2. A Sea of Forgiveness
   "*He will turn again, he will have compassion upon us; he will subdue our iniquities; and thou wilt cast all their sins into the depths of the sea.*" Micah 7:19

3. A Sea of Victory
   "*And I saw as it were a sea of glass mingled with fire: and them that had gotten the <u>victory over the beast, and over his image, and over his mark, and over the number of his name</u>, stand on the sea of glass, having the harps of God.*" Revelation 15:2

4. A Sea of Steadfast Faith
   "*And I saw as it were a sea of glass mingled with fire: and them that had gotten the victory over the beast, and over his image, and over his mark, and over the number of his name, <u>stand on the sea of glass</u>, having the harps of God.*" Revelation 15:2

5. A Sea of Harmonious Praise in Worship
   "*And I saw as it were a sea of glass mingled with fire: and them that had gotten the victory over the beast, and over his image, and over his mark, and over the number of his name, stand on the sea of glass, <u>having the harps of God</u>.*" Revelation 15:2

6. The Sea of Glass as the Light of Truth
   "*Having the glory of God: and her light was like unto a stone most precious, even like a jasper stone, clear as crystal;*" Revelation 21:11

III. A SEA OF GLASS: THE CENTRAL TRUTH

1. "*...in the midst of the throne,*"

The Gospel of Christ, who He is and what He has done is the central truth of Christ's reign

2. *"For I determined not to know any thing among you, save Jesus Christ, and him crucified."* 1 Corinthians 2:2

IV. A SEA OF GLASS: THE WONDER OF HEAVEN

1. *"...and round about the throne, were four beasts full of eyes before and behind."*

The priority and preeminence of the Gospel of Jesus Christ strikes the heavenly host with awe

2. *"For after that in the wisdom of God the world by wisdom knew not God, it pleased God by the foolishness of preaching to save them that believe."* 1 Corinthians 1:21

3. *"Unto whom it was revealed, that not unto themselves, but unto us they did minister the things, which are now reported unto you by them that have preached the gospel unto you with the Holy Ghost sent down from heaven; which things the angels desire to look into."* 1 Peter 3:12

Outline Seven

The Lamb Opens the Seals

I. INTRODUCTION

Preeminence & Priorities from our Divine Outline:

    1. Christ in Revelation
        — The Lord Seen (Prophet), Rev 1:1-3

    2. Christ in Salvation
        — The Lamb Slain (Priest), Rev 1:4-6

    3. Christ in Sanctification
        — The Light Supreme (King), Rev 1:7-20

Passage for our Outline Selection
Revelation 6:1-7:17

    1. Seals Opening: a Celebrated Narration
       (an Historic Interpretation)

    2. Seals Opening: a Special Revelation
       (a Personal Salvation)

3. Seals Opening: a Future Consummation?

II. A CELEBRATED NARRATION

  1st Seal: Corruption (Depravity)

  2nd Seal: Conflict (Disparity)

  3rd Seal: Curse (Dearth)

  4th Seal: Close (Death)

  5th Seal: Cry of the Prophets

  6th Seal: Coming of Christ

  7th Seal: Sanctification by Christ (ch.8)

III. A SPECIAL REVELATION

  1st Seal: Slaves to Sin

  2nd Seal: Separated from God

  3rd Seal: Suffering in the World

  4th Seal: Sentence in Judgment

  5th Seal: Saints' Witness

  6th Seal: Salvation in Christ

  7th Seal: Sanctification by, in, & through Christ

Sermon Outlines for Revelation

IV. A FUTURE CONSUMMATION?

1st Seal: Fall of Man to Exalt Antichrist

2nd Seal: Flesh vs. Spirit, Enmity against Christ

3rd Seal: Futility of Man's Labors in Efforts on a Cursed Earth

4th Seal: Final End in Execution of Judgment

5th Seal: Faithful Brethren to the End

6th Seal: Fury of Christ

7th Seal: Fast (quick) Coming of Christ (ch.8)

Outline Eight

The Praise of Sovereign Grace

I. REVELATION 7:9, 10

"After this I beheld, and, lo, a great multitude, which no man could number, of all nations, and kindreds, and people, and tongues, stood before the throne, and before the Lamb, clothed with white robes, and palms in their hands; And cried with a loud voice, saying, Salvation to our God which sitteth upon the throne, and unto the Lamb."

II. AFTER THIS...

Μετα ταυτα
The term occurs in Rev 4:1; 7:1; 7:9; 9:2; 15:5; 18:1; 19:1

    A Greek term that can mean:

    —"After this" (in chronology, with respect to time)
    —"Along with" (in space, with regard to proximity)
    —"While that" (in relation, with regard to action)

III. MULTITUDES

The Praise of Sovereign Grace

    1. Great tribulation

    2. All nations, kindreds...

    3. Before the throne (present & future)

    4. White robes

    5. Palms

III. PRAISE

    1. Sovereignty of God

    2. Gospel of God

Outline Nine

I. INTRODUCTION

    Revelation of Jesus Christ
        — the gospel supremely expressed

    Revelation of St. John the Divine
        — the gospel submissively possessed

    Rev 1:19. Scroll, Trumpets, Vials

    Rev 5. True Spiritual Worship:
        — Word & Prayer unto Praise

    Rev 6, 7. The Word of the Lamb Revealed

Passage for our Outline Selection

    Revelation 8:1-9:21

II. IN PREPARATION, Revelation 8:1-6

    1. Holy importance, vv1-2

    2. Heavenly intercessions, vv3-4

    3. Holy impact, vv5-6

    4. Numbers 10:2-10

    5. Ephesians 6:10-18

III. FIRST FOUR TRUMPETS, Revelation 8:7-13

    1. The Ramifications of Sin

    2. The Reality of Judgment

IV. FIRST TWO WOES, Rev 9:1-21

    1. The Fifth Trumpet (Woe #1), vv1-12

    2. The Sixth Trumpet (Woe #2), vv13-21

Outline Ten

I. INTRODUCTION

Revelation of Jesus Christ
— the gospel supremely expressed

Revelation of St. John the Divine
— the gospel submissively possessed

Rev 4. Heavenly Wonder
— the Lamb upon His Throne

Rev 5. True Spiritual Worship
— Word & Prayer unto Praise

Rev 6, 7. The Word of the Lamb Revealed

Rev 8, 9. The Sounds of Warfare Trumpeted

Passage for our Outline Selection

Revelation 10:1-11:19

II. THE GOSPEL PROCLAIMED, Revelation 10:1-11:14

   1. Another Mighty Angel, 10:1-7

   2. The Little Book, 10:8-11

   3. Conformity to Christ, 11:1-2

   4. Witnesses of Grace, 11:3-8

   5. Work of the Gospel, 11:9-14

   6. Reference: Matthew 16:24-28

III. THE GOSPEL PRAISED, Revelation 11:15-19

   1. The Seventh Trumpet Sounds (the Third Woe), v15a

   2. The Praise of Heaven, v15b

   3. The Praise of Saints, vv16-18

   4. The Power of the Gospel, v19

IV. THE GOSPEL PREVAILS, Revelation 12-14

   1. Rev 12, The Incarnation: Enmity twixt the serpent & the woman, Gen 3:15a

   2. Rev 13, The Curse of Corruption: Enmity twixt the serpent's seed & seed of the woman, Gen 3:15b

   3. Rev 14, The Conquering Lamb: Bruising the Seed's heel in bruising the serpent's head, Gen 3:15

Outline Eleven

A Wonder in Heaven

I. INTRODUCTION

    Revelation of Jesus Christ
        —the gospel supremely expressed

    Revelation of St. John the Divine
        —the gospel submissively possessed

    Rev 2, 3. Letters to the Seven Churches
        —Sufficiency in the Lamb
        —Reward is the Lamb

    Rev 4. Heavenly Wonder
        —the Lamb upon His Throne

    Rev 5. True Spiritual Worship
        —Word & Prayer unto Praise

    Rev 6, 7. The Word of the Lamb Revealed

    Rev 8, 9. The Sounds of Warfare Trumpeted

Rev 10, 11. The Gospel Proclaimed & Praised

IA. INTRODUCTION CONTINUED: The Prevailing Gospel

1. Revelation 12, The Incarnation
— Enmity twixt the serpent & the woman, Gen 3:15

2. Revelation 13, The Curse of Corruption
— Enmity twixt the serpent's seed & seed of the woman, Gen 3:15

3. Revelation 14, The Conquering Lamb
— Bruising the Seed's heel in bruising the serpent's head, Gen 3:15

4. Reference: *"And I will put enmity between thee and the woman, and between thy seed and her seed; it shall bruise thy head, and thou shalt bruise his heel."* Genesis 3:15

Passage for our Outline Selection

Revelation 12:1-17

II. THE VIRGIN BIRTH, Revelation 12:1-5

And I will put enmity between… thy seed and her seed…

III. AUTHORITY CRUSHED, Revelation 12:6-10

…it shall bruise thy head…

IV. THE CROSS OF CHRIST, Revelation 12:11-12

Sermon Outlines for Revelation

...shalt bruise his heel.

V. SATAN'S WAR AGAINST THE CHURCH, Revelation 12:13-17

...enmity between thee and the woman...

Outline Twelve

The Mark of the Beast

I. INTRODUCTION

    Revelation of Jesus Christ
        — the gospel supremely expressed

    Revelation of St. John the Divine
        — the gospel submissively possessed

    Rev 2, 3. Letters to the Seven Churches
        — Sufficiency in the Lamb
        — Reward is the Lamb

    Rev 4. Heavenly Wonder
        — the Lamb upon His Throne

    Rev 5. True Spiritual Worship
        — Word & Prayer unto Praise

    Rev 6, 7. The Seals of the Word Opened
        — Christ as Prophet

The Mark of the Beast

Rev 8, 9. The Sounds of Warfare Trumpeted
— Christ as Priest

Rev 10, 11. The Gospel Proclaimed & Praised
— Christ as King, reigning by & through the Gospel

The Prevailing Gospel:

Rev 12. The Incarnation
— Enmity twixt the serpent & the woman, Gen 3:15

Rev 13. The Curse of Corruption
— Enmity twixt the serpent's seed & seed of the woman, Gen 3:15

Rev 14. The Conquering Lamb
— Bruising the Seed's heel in bruising the serpent's head, Gen 3:15

Passage for our Outline Selection

Revelation 13:1-18

II. THE BEAST FROM THE SEA, Revelation 13:1-10

1. Fallen mankind…
— The Gospel (Sea of Glass) provides a recognizable distinction between the reprobate and redeemed

III. THE BEAST FROM THE EARTH, Revelation 13:11-14

Sermon Outlines for Revelation

1. False Prophets…

IV. THE IMAGE OF THE BEAST, Revelation 13:14-15
1. Every thought and imagination only evil continually…
— (see Genesis 6:5)

V. THE MARK OF THE BEAST, Revelation 13:15-18

1. Indicates worship of anything other than Christ, v15

2. Indicts & desires to kill true worship of Christ, v15

3. The mark is represents, v16:
— fallen man's best works (right hand)
— fallen man's best thoughts (forehead)

4. Will it dominate every aspect of society in its corruption? v17

5. The Beast's Mark is pride, idolatry & adultery, v18
— thrice unholy
— thrice defiant
— thrice short of God's glory

Outline Thirteen

The Lamb Slain

"And all that dwell upon the earth shall worship him, whose names are not written in the book of life of the Lamb slain from the foundation of the world." **—Revelation 13:8**

I. ETERNAL TRUTH

    1. The Lamb Slain is Eternal Truth
        —"*the Lamb slain from the foundation of the world.*"

    2. "*Forasmuch as ye know that ye were not redeemed with corruptible things, as silver and gold, from your vain conversation received by tradition from your fathers; But with the precious blood of Christ, as of a lamb without blemish and without spot: Who verily was foreordained before the foundation of the world, but was manifest in these last times for you,*" 1 Peter 1:18-20

II. ETERNAL LIFE

    1. The Lamb Slain gives Eternal Life

—"*whose names are not written in the book of life of the Lamb slain*"
—The names of idolaters and adulterers blotted out of the book of life stands in contrast to the eternal reality of those who have received the grace of God to own life in Christ.

2. Eternal life belongs to all those who worship Christ, "*He that hath the Son hath life; and he that hath not the Son of God hath not life.*" 1 John 5:12

III. ETERNAL WORSHIP

1. The Lamb Slain produces Eternal Worship
—"*And all that dwell upon the earth shall worship him*" The temporal worship of idolaters and adulterers is contrasted by the eternal worship of those in Christ.

2. "*And there shall be no night there; and they need no candle, neither light of the sun; for the Lord God giveth them light: and they shall reign for ever and ever.*" Revelation 22:5

Outline Fourteen

The Lamb on the Mount Sion

I. INTRODUCTION

    Revelation of Jesus Christ
        —the gospel supremely expressed

    Revelation of St. John the Divine
        —the gospel submissively possessed

    Rev 2, 3. Letters to the Seven Churches
        —Sufficiency in the Lamb
        —Reward is the Lamb

    Rev 4. Heavenly Wonder
        —the Lamb upon His Throne

    Rev 5. Heavenly Worship
        —Word & Prayer unto Praise

    Rev 6, 7. The Seals of the Word Opened
        —Christ as Prophet

The Lamb on the Mount Sion

Rev 8, 9. The Sounds of Warfare Trumpeted
— Christ as Priest

Rev 10, 11. The Gospel Proclaimed & Praised
— Christ as King, reigning by & through the Gospel

The Prevailing Gospel:

Rev 12. The Incarnation
— Enmity twixt the serpent & the woman, Gen 3:15

Rev 13. The Curse of Corruption
— Enmity twixt the serpent's seed & seed of the woman, Gen 3:15

Rev 14. The Conquering Lamb
— Bruising the Seed's heel in bruising the serpent's head, Gen 3:15

Passage for our Outline Selection

Revelation 14:1-5

II. THE LAMB ON THE MOUNT, Revelation 14:1

1. Sion/Zion: the Man condemned to die

2. Sion/Zion: the Lamb conquering sin and death

III. THE LAMB LEADS HIS SAINTS, Revelation 14:1-5

1. 144,000

Sermon Outlines for Revelation

2. Name of God on their minds

3. Perfect praise from Word & prayer
4. Virgins, undefiled

5. Follows the Lamb everywhere

6. Firstfruits of Christ

7. No guile in their mouths

8. Without fault

Outline Fifteen

I. INTRODUCTION

    Revelation of Jesus Christ
        — the gospel supremely expressed

    Revelation of St. John the Divine
        — the gospel submissively possessed

    Rev 2, 3. Letters to the Seven Churches
        — Sufficiency in the Lamb
        — Reward is the Lamb

    Rev 4. Heavenly Wonder
        — the Lamb upon His Throne

    Rev 5. Heavenly Worship
        — Word & Prayer unto Praise

    Rev 6, 7. The Seals of the Word Opened
        — Christ as Prophet

Rev 8, 9. The Sounds of Warfare Trumpeted
— Christ as Priest

Rev 10, 11. The Gospel Proclaimed & Praised
— Christ as King, reigning by & through the Gospel

The Prevailing Gospel:

Rev 12. The Incarnation
— Enmity twixt the serpent & the woman, Gen 3:15

Rev 13. The Curse of Corruption
— Enmity twixt the serpent's seed & seed of the woman, Gen 3:15

Rev 14. The Conquering Lamb
— Bruising the Seed's heel in bruising the serpent's head, Gen 3:15
— Rev 14:1, The Lamb victoriously stands upon His Sion
— Rev 14:1-5, The Lamb gloriously leads His Saints

Passage for our Outline Selection

Revelation 14:6-20

II. THE LAMB'S HOLY JUDGMENT, Revelation 14:6-11

1. By divine proclamation, vv6-7

2. Through destruction of the evil city, vv8-9

3. In determined wrath upon wicked men, vv10-11

III. THE LAMB'S HOLY HARVEST, Revelation 14:12-20

    1. By patient faith on Jesus Christ, v12

    2. By a witness unto death in Christ, v13

    3. By the grace of God alone in Christ, vv14-16

    4. By the witness of the shed blood of Christ, through the witness of His martyred saints, vv17-20

Outline Sixteen

The Wrath of God

I. INTRODUCTION

    Revelation of Jesus Christ
        — the gospel supremely expressed

    Revelation of St. John the Divine
        — the gospel submissively possessed

    Rev 2, 3. Letters to the Seven Churches
        — Sufficiency in the Lamb
        — Reward is the Lamb

    Rev 4. Heavenly Wonder
        — the Lamb upon His Throne

    Rev 5. Heavenly Worship
        — Word & Prayer unto Praise

    Rev 6, 7. The Seals of the Word Opened
        — Christ as Prophet

The Wrath of God

    Rev 8, 9. The Sounds of Warfare Trumpeted
        —Christ as Priest

    Rev 10, 11. The Gospel Proclaimed & Praised
        —Christ as King, reigning by & through the Gospel

The Prevailing Gospel:

    Rev 12. The Incarnation
        —Enmity twixt the serpent & the woman, Gen 3:15

    Rev 13. The Curse of Corruption
        —Enmity twixt the serpent's seed & seed of the woman, Gen 3:15

    Rev 14. The Conquering Lamb
        —Bruising the Seed's heel in bruising the serpent's head, Gen 3:15
        —Rev 14:1, The Lamb victoriously stands upon His Sion
        —Rev 14:1-5, The Lamb gloriously leads His Saints
        —Rev 14:6-11, The Lamb's holy judgments
        —Rev 14:12-20, The Lamb's holy harvest

    Rev 15. The Righteous Lamb
        —Christ as Judge
        —The wrath of God revealed from heaven…
            —Romans 1:18

Passage for our Outline Selection

Sermon Outlines for Revelation

Revelation 15:1-8

II. A SIGN IN HEAVEN, v1

    1. Seven Angels
       —a message complete

    2. Seven Last Plagues
       —a justice fulfilled

III. THE SONG OF SAINTS, vv2-4

    1. The Gospel honored, v2

    2. The Gospel of Law and Grace harmonized, v3

    3. The Glory of God held high, v4

IV. THE SMOKE OF GLORY, vv5-8

    1. The testimony of grace divinely displayed, v5

    2. The temple of grace dispatches her messengers, v6

    3. The truth of God delegated in holiness, v7

    4. The terror of God dispensed in the fullness of glory, v8

Outline Seventeen

Seven Vials & Mystery Babylon

I. INTRODUCTION, Christ-centered Judgment

    Rev 15. The Righteous Lamb

    Rev 16. The Wrath of God Outpoured

    Rev 17. The Wrath of God Explained

Passage for our Outline Selection

    Revelation 16:1-17:18

II. COMMAND TO THE SEVEN ANGELS, Revelation 16:1-14

    1. **Vial One**: visible corruption upon "marked" idolaters & adulterers (note that pride is merely self-idolatry)

    2. **Vial Two**: the gospel (sea) that gives life by the blood of Christ, becomes blood and death to all those who have rejected the Christ of the gospel.

3. **Vial Three**: the living water of the Holy Spirit (rivers and fountains: John 7:38; James 3:11) provides no illumination of the gospel and no effectual call of the gospel, this judgment bringing only death to all those who have rejected God's Christ.

4. **Vial Four**: the darkness of their evil is poured out so that there is not even any natural light to illuminate the way to life and through life. Evil men burned with only one desire, to fulfill the passions of their own lusts (Romans 1:24-25).

5. **Vial Five**: God gave them up unto their vile affections and their sins against nature, which was the very seat of their perversions and earthly kingdom (Romans 1:26-27).

6. **Vial Six**: God gave them over to a reprobate mind, to do those things which are not convenient (Romans 1:28-32), their souls being ruled by corrupt, sinful and earthly authorities and dominions, who give no glory or reverence to the God of heaven.

III. CHRIST COMES AS A THIEF, 16:15

"Thief" κλεπτης (*kleptees*)
 — Where we get the word kleptomaniac, the Greek word used of an embezzler.
 — References: Rev 3:3; Matt 24:43; 1 Thess 5:2-3; 2 Pet 3:10

IV. CORRUPT BABYLON DESTROYED, 16:16-21

Sermon Outlines for Revelation

Vial Seven: God's final judgment upon the entire city of fallen, God-hating, Christ-rejecting me.

V. THE WHORE ON MANY WATERS, 17:1-2

1. The whore is any and every false religious system
   — In contrast to the Bride of Christ

2. Many waters are the multitude of voices that promote and proclaim her grace-denying, faith-rebelling false gospel (Rev 17:15).

VI. THE WOMAN ON A BEAST IN THE WILDERNESS, 17:3-6

1. This woman, this false religious system, was not carried along by the Spirit of Christ, but instead, rode upon the pride, idolatry and adultery of fallen men, which was full of blasphemy against God. 17:3

2. The false religious systems rode upon the work of the old dragon, Satan (Revelation 12:9), who assumed complete authority (seven heads), and established obedience and allegiance to the lies of his kingdom (ten horns). 17:3

3. This woman was adorned with clothing and precious jewels like Christ's church, but was instead, full of pride, idolatry, and uncleanness. 17:4

4. Upon her forehead, 17:5... *"And GOD saw that the wickedness of man was great in the earth, and that every imagination of the thoughts of his heart was only evil continually."* Genesis 6:5

5. Her ways and wickedness brings death to the saints of God in Christ. 17:6

VII. THE WISDOM REVEALED IN THE BEAST, 17:7-17

1. The beast's description is Satanic, 17:7-8 (Revelation 12:3-12)

2. The beast's identity has been displayed in the kingdoms of men, 17:9-12

3. The beast's power is reliant upon the corrupt wisdom of vain philosophy, 17:12-13

4. The beast opposes the Lamb, His sheep, and His gospel, 17:14

5. The beast's kingdoms (ten horns) spring forth from the beast and are a part of the beast; and they hate the whore, who is only a rider and a loathsome burden. 17:16

6. The judgments from God are ordained by His through His sovereignty to be executed by their own wickedness.

VIII. THE WISDOM REVEALED IN THE WOMAN, 17:18

1. The woman is described as a city, a habitation of people.

2. This false religious system rules over corrupt earthly authorities.

Outline Eighteen

Mystery Babylon & the Beast

I. INTRODUCTION, Christ-centered Judgment

    Rev 15. The Righteous Lamb

    Rev 16. The Wrath of God Outpoured

    Rev 17. The Wrath of God Explained

Passage for our Outline Selection

    Revelation 17:1-18

II. THE WHORE ON MANY WATERS, 17:1-2

    1. Harlot = apostate church, v1a

    2. Many waters: Influence spans the nations of the world (see v15) v1b

    3. The EXPANSE of Her Apostasy (vv1-2), distance

4. The EXTENT of Her Apostasy (vv3-6), depth

III. THE WOMAN ON A BEAST IN THE WILDERNESS, 17:3-6

1. Wilderness. Apostate church is in the wilderness, as the true church (Rev 12:6, 14), v3a

2. Beast. Similar to Satan, Rev 12:3-6 & same basic description as his antichrist (Rev 13:1), v3b
   — 7 heads; 10 horns; names of blasphemy: Rev 13:1, 5

3. Scarlet Beast. v3c

4. Woman arrayed. v4

5. Mother of Harlots (fornication). Her adultery begets adultery. v5

6. Woman drunken with murder v6

IV. THE WISDOM REVEALED IN THE BEAST, 17:7-17

1. The Beast
   — PAST v8a "was" John 8:44
   — PRESENT (John's Day) v8b "is not" Rev 12.9; Luke 10:18
   — FUTURE v8c "shall ascend" 2 Thess 2:3

2. "seven mountains" v10 tells not mountains, vv9-10, but "kings" Dan 2:31-35
   — fallen: Egypt, Assyria, Babylon, Medo-Persian, Greece

— *"one is"* =Rome
   — *"one is yet to come"* = worldwide... 10 iron/miry clay toes from two legs

   3. Satan's man, the beast antichrist, is possessed of Satan. v11

   4. Ten kings correspond to the 10 toes of Daniel 2. v12

   5. Satan, antichrist, false prophet... are mutually minded, & at times mutually described. v13

   6. Hatred for the Lord & his people. vv14-16 (John 15:18)

   7. v17 corresponds with the 5th vial (Rev 16:10-11)

V. THE WISDOM REVEALED IN THE WOMAN, 17:18

   1. Two cities
      — Babylon vs. Jerusalem
      — City of Destruction vs. Celestial city
      — Hebrews 11:8-10

Outline Nineteen

Babylon is Fallen

I. INTRODUCTION & OVERVIEW

    Rev 15. The Wrath of God Anticipated

    Rev 16. The Wrath of God Outpoured

    Rev 17. The Wrath of God Explained

    Rev 18. The Wrath of God Considered

Passage for our Outline Selection

    Revelation 18:1-24

II. A CITY DESTROYED, vv1-3

    1. The gospel is from heaven by condescending grace, v1a

    2. The gospel message is great and powerful, v1b

3. The gospel message exposes God's judgment to come, v2

4. The gospel message exposes men's sins, v3

III. A COMMAND TO DEPART, vv4-7

1. The gospel message effectually calls God's people to fly from the wrath to come, v4

2. The sins of men cannot be hidden from God, v5

3. Even a double portion of their own sins poured out upon them, is still gracious in their evil and wickedness against a good, holy and infinite God, v6

4. The sins of pride, idolatry and uncleanness are self-deceiving and delusional, v7

IV. A CRY FROM THE DEPRAVED, vv8-19

1. The final judgment upon Babylon is immediate, in "one day," v8; and in "one hour," v17

2. Sinful men, merchants and monarchs bewail the destruction of Babylon, vv9-19

V. A COMMAND TO DELIGHT, vv20-24

1. When the wretched depravity of sin is revealed for the enmity against a holy God, God's justice is a truth of rejoicing and worthy of praise.

Outline Twenty

Two Suppers

I. INTRODUCTION & OVERVIEW

    Rev 15. The Wrath of God Anticipated

    Rev 16. The Wrath of God Outpoured

    Rev 17. The Wrath of God Explained
       — A Tale of Two Gospels

    Rev 18. The Wrath of God Considered
       — A Tale of Two Cities

    Rev 19. The Wrath of God Revealed
       — A Tale of Two Suppers

Passage for our Outline Selection

Revelation 19:1-21

1st Supper: Christ's Wedding Observed

II. THE WORSHIP OF GOD IN HEAVEN, vv1-6

1. Great Whore (apostate church; prostituted religion), vv1-3

2. The heavenly host worships God in spiritual truth, v4

3. The Lamb from the throne commands praise of God of all his subjects, v5

4. The redeemed of every kindred, tongue, people & nation, v6

III. THE WIFE OF THE LAMB IN LINEN, vv7-10

Praise continues with the marriage of the Lamb

1. Christ's wife has made herself ready, v7
— Ephesians 5:25-27; Romans 12:1-2

2. Christ's wife is clothed with Christ's righteousness by faith, v8
— Romans 3:21-22

3. *"And he saith unto me, Write,"* v9a
— Habakkuk 2:2-4

4. *"Blessed are they which are called unto the marriage supper of the Lamb."* v9b
— Matthew 22:1-14

5. *"And he saith unto me, These are the true sayings of God."* v9c
— Titus 3:8

6. *"…worship God: for the testimony of Jesus is the spirit of prophecy."* v10
    —John 5:39

2nd Supper: Christ's Wrath Outpoured

IV. THE WORD OF GOD IN TRIUMPH, vv11-16

    1. v11, in contrast to Revelation 6:2

    2. v12, Judges 13:8

    3. v13, Isaiah 63:1-3

    4. v14, (v8)

    5. v15, His judgment comes by the truth of His Word

    6. v16, 1 Timothy 6:14-15

V. THE WRATH OF GOD IN JUDGMENT, vv17-21

    1. Matthew 24:27-28

    2. Revelation 16:15-21

Outline Twenty-One

"And I fell at his feet to worship him. And he said unto me, See thou do it not: I am thy fellowservant, and of thy brethren that have the testimony of Jesus: worship God: for the testimony of Jesus is the spirit of prophecy." —**Revelation 19:10**

I. THE WITNESS OF CHRIST

    A. *"testimony of Jesus"*
        —Christ is the fulfillment of all prophecy, John 5:39
        —Christ is the embodiment of all prophecy, Colossians 2:9
        —Christ is the express image of all prophecy, Hebrews 1:3

2. The Worship of God
    A. *"worship God"*
        —The witness of Christ produces worship, Philippians 3:3

3. The Word's of Christ's Servant

A. *"I am thy fellowservant"*
 — The testimony of Christ by the redeemed comes by cleansing power of the blood, *"And they overcame him by the blood of the Lamb, and by the word of their testimony; and they loved not their lives unto the death."* Revelation 12:11

Outline Twenty-Two

Two Resurrections

I. INTRODUCTION & OVERVIEW

    Rev 15. The Wrath of God Anticipated

    Rev 16. The Wrath of God Outpoured

    Rev 17. The Wrath of God Explained

    Rev 18. The Wrath of God Considered

    Rev 19. The Wrath of God Revealed

    Rev 20. The Wrath of God Completed

Passage for our Outline Selection

    Revelation 20:1-15

II. THE RESTRAINT OF SATAN, vv1-3

    1. Restrained for the gospel to go to all nations, v1

2. Restrained for a long time, vv2-3
   — a thousand years is not specified, one thousand or two thousand, but simply, χιλια ετη
   — 2 Peter 3:8

III. THE RESURRECTION UNTO SALVATION, vv4-6

   1. Ruling and reigning with Christ
      — Ephesians 2:6

IV. THE RELEASE OF SATAN, vv7-10

   1. The free proclamation of the gospel will be subdued with the release of Satan

V. THE RESURRECTION UNTO JUDGMENT, vv11-15

   1. The return of Christ will end Satan's final thrust

   2. The dead will be raised unto judgment

Sermon Outlines for Revelation

sermons preached from these notes are available at SermonAudio.com

go to

www.sermonaudio.com/vayahiy

About the Author

"For I determined not to know any thing among you, save Jesus Christ, and him crucified."

1 Corinthians 2:2

Jon J. Cardwell is a wretched sinner saved by God's free and sovereign grace. He lives in Anniston, Alabama with his wife, Lisa, his daughter, Rachel, and his mother-in-law, Virginia. He is the pastor at Sovereign Grace Baptist Church in Anniston after having ministered as a missionary and as a missionary-pastor in the Philippines, California, and remote bush Alaska.

He is the author of the bestseller, *Christ and Him Crucified*, the CEO of Vayahiy Press, and the founder and overseer of Free Grace Tentmakers. Jon has also held the office of vice-chairman of the national Sovereign Grace Baptist Fellowship (2009-11), was elected as chairman on September 13, 2011, and reelected September 11, 2012.

His Christianity has been shaped tremendously and influenced deeply by such redeemed sinners as John Bunyan (1628-1688), Charles H. Spurgeon (1834-1892), John Newton (1725-1807), and Granville Gauldin (1929-).

Other titles by Jon include *A Puritan Family Devotional*, *Fullness of the Time*, *Lord Teach Us to Pray*, *Master Mega Writing*, and *Powerful Gospel Grace*.

> CHRIST AND HIM CRUCIFIED
> *workbooks will be available soon.*
>
> *for*
> CHRIST AND HIM CRUCIFIED
> *seminars, workshops or speaking engagements, as well as those on worship, family devotions, and catechizing, you can contact Jon J. Cardwell through:*
>
> **SOVEREIGN GRACE BAPTIST CHURCH**
> 5440 AL Hwy 202 ~ Anniston, AL 36201
> Phone: (256) 275-8996
> Email: jon@justificationbygrace.com

Check Out Jon J. Cardwell on the Web

jonjcardwell.net

jonjcardwell.info

jonjcardwell.biz

vayahiypress.com

justificationbygrace.com

sovereigngraceanniston.com

www.facebook.com/Vayahiy.Press

www.twitter.com/vayahiy

www.pinterest.com/jonjcardwell

Fiction for Youth

YOU KILL'D MY PAHDER, FREFARE TO DIE

Currently available is novella for young adults,

YOU KILL'D MY PAHDER, FREFARE TO DIE

THE CONTINUING SAGA & DELICIOUS MISADVENTURES OF
WILMER P. COHEN: PILGRIM, PATRIOT, JUST PLAIN JOE

Check Us Out...

On the Web
youkilledmypahder.com

On Facebook
www.facebook.com/WilmerP.Cohen

On Twitter
www.twitter.com/WilmerPCohen

On YouTube
www.youtube.com/YouKilldMyPahder

At Our Blog
youkilledmypahder.info

COMING SOON

COMMENTARY SERIES IN ROMANS

PROFITABLE GOSPEL FAITH (Romans 4-6)
PROVOKING GOSPEL LOVE (Romans 7-8)
PROVIDENTIAL GOSPEL LORDSHIP (Romans 9-12)
PRACTICAL GOSPEL STEWARDSHIP (Romans 13-15)
PASSIONATE GOSPEL FELLOWSHIP (Romans 1, 6)

POWERFUL GOSPEL GRACE (Romans 1-3) is already available in paperback and Kindle eBook at Amazon.com

NEVERTHELESS I LIVE

This is the sequel to *Christ and Him Crucified*, expected to be launched in paperback and Kindle in 2013.
http://neverthelessilive.com

CHRIST REVEALED

This is a commentary which presents the glorious gospel throughout the book of Revelation, expected to be launched in 2013. Sign up to receive updates on its release at,
http://christ-revealed.com

Coming Soon

SERMON OUTLINES FOR GENESIS

Similar in format to this book, *Sermon Outlines for Genesis* come from the sermons, messages and devotionals preached by Jon Cardwell in 2011, and is expected to be available in paperback and Kindle in 2013.
http://genesis.sermonoutlinesbook.com

SERMON OUTLINES FOR MARK'S GOSPEL

Similar in format to this book, *Sermon Outlines for Mark's Gospel* come from the sermons, messages and devotionals preached by Jon Cardwell in 2012, and is expected to be available in paperback and Kindle in 2013.
http://mark.sermonoutlinesbook.com

HAB PUN STORMING THE CASTLE

This is the exciting sequel to the young adult fiction, *You Kill'd My Pahder, Frefare to Die*. This picks up where the first book left off, and is filled with even more action and adventure in the continuing saga of Wilmer P. Cohen.
http://habpunstormingthecastle.com

WHEN JESUS WAS BORN

Was Jesus born in the fall or the winter? Or was it the spring? What is the Biblical evidence to support any view? Is there anything wrong with celebrating or observing Christmas? These questions and more are answered in this book, expected out approximately Thanksgiving 2013.
http://whenjesuswasborn.com

Made in United States
Orlando, FL
21 March 2023